WILLIAMS-SONOMA

FOODMADEFAST
small plates

RECIPES

Brigit L. Binns

GENERAL EDITOR

Chuck Williams

PHOTOGRAPHY

Tucker & Hossler

Oxmoor House®

contents

20 MINUTES START TO FINISH

10 walnut crostini with gorgonzola & pear

13 citrus-marinated olives

14 pear compote with cheeses

17 white bean dip with pita

18 ricotta, fig & prosciutto bruschetta

21 radishes with butter & sea salt

22 salmon & herbed cheese pinwheels

25 spiced roasted nuts

26 caprese skewers

29 thai lettuce cups

30 turkey & manchego sandwiches

33 fried garbanzos

34 crab salad with endive

37 chorizo & cheese quesadillas

38 goat cheese stuffed tomatoes

41 peaches with prosciutto & mint

30 MINUTES START TO FINISH

44 crostini with steak & horseradish cream

47 guacamole & sweet potato chips

48 spring rolls with lime-cilantro sauce

51 grilled pork with pineapple salsa

52 shrimp skewers with basil oil

55 lamb meatballs with cilantro raita

56 artichokes with lemon aioli

59 fritto misto

60 potato pancakes with smoked salmon

63 roasted dates with parmesan & bacon

64 tamarind-glazed chicken wings

67 gruyère-chive popovers

68 ceviche with mango & avocado

71 polenta with eggplant pesto

72 tomatillo gazpacho

75 lemon chicken salad on crostini

MAKE MORE TO STORE

78 flatbread with rosemary & olive oil

81 pesto & cherry tomato pizza

83 pancetta, ricotta & spinach calzone

85 olive & onion pissaladière

86 tomato & fontina tart

89 ham & spinach quiches

90 mushroom & mascarpone tartlets

93 beef empanadas

95 the smarter cook

103 the well-stocked kitchen

108 index

about this book

Food Made Fast *Small Plates* is perfect for busy people who love to entertain. The delicious recipes found in this book are simple enough for the most casual get-together yet elegant enough for a stylish affair. These easy-to-prepare appetizers allow you to spend less time in the kitchen and more time enjoying yourself with your family and friends.

You will also find helpful, time-saving tips on presentation that will minimize any last-minute pressure in the kitchen and help create the perfect mood for entertaining. Such impressive dishes as Grilled Pork with Pineapple Salsa or Polenta with Eggplant Pesto can be prepared in 30 minutes, while Thai Lettuce Cups can be ready in under 20 minutes. This collection of recipes offers proof that preparing crowd-pleasing food is just a matter of being well organized, shopping smarter, and using straightforward recipes.

20 minutes
start to finish

walnut crostini with gorgonzola & pear

Walnut bread, 7 slices, crusts trimmed, if desired

Gorgonzola cheese, 7 oz (220 g), at room temperature

Pear, 1, quartered, cored, and thinly sliced

Salt and freshly ground pepper

MAKES ABOUT
14 CROSTINI

1 **Assemble the crostini**
Cut each slice of bread in half crosswise. Spread the cheese evenly on each bread slice and top with two thin slices of pear. Transfer the crostini to a platter, sprinkle with salt and pepper, and serve.

cook's tip

Store marinated olives in a jar
or an airtight container for
up to 1 month in the refrigerator.
The longer the olives marinate
the better, as the flavors will
continue to develop over time.

citrus-marinated olives

1 Marinate the olives
In a clean 1½ cup (375-ml) jar, combine the olives, fennel seeds, orange zest and juice, garlic, pepper flakes, peppercorns, and olive oil. Cover and shake the jar to compact the ingredients. The contents should reach within about 1 inch (2.5 cm) of the rim. Uncover and add water until the ingredients are just covered. Shake the jar to release any air bubbles. The olive oil will rise to the top. Cover and let marinate for at least 15 minutes.

2 Serve the olives
Using a slotted spoon, transfer the olives to a serving bowl, discarding the liquid in the jar. Serve the olives alongside a small bowl to dispose of the pits.

Brine-cured green olives such as Manzanillo, 1 lb (500 g), drained

Fennel seeds, 2 tablespoons

Finely grated zest and juice from 1 orange

Garlic, 2 cloves, thinly sliced

Red pepper flakes, ½ teaspoon

Peppercorns, 10

Olive oil, 3 tablespoons

MAKES ABOUT
60 OLIVES

pear compote
with cheeses

Pears such as Bartlett (Williams') or Bosc, 2, peeled, quartered, cored, and coarsely chopped

Star anise or cinnamon stick, 1

Fruity white wine such as Riesling, 2½ tablespoons

Sugar, 1 tablespoon, or to taste

Aged pecorino cheese, 4 oz (125 g)

Maytag or other blue cheese, 4 oz (125 g)

Toasted crostini (page 70) or large crackers

MAKES ABOUT
24 PIECES

1 Cook the pears and seasoning
In a frying pan over medium-low heat, combine the pears, star anise, wine, and sugar. Bring to a gentle simmer and cook, stirring occasionally, until the pears are almost falling apart, about 12 minutes. Let cool to warm room temperature. (The compote may be refrigerated for up to 8 hours; bring it to room temperature before serving.)

2 Arrange the platter
Transfer the compote to a bowl and place on a large platter. Arrange the cheeses and crostini around the compote. Layer a slice of cheese and a dollop of compote on each crostini and serve.

(Toasted crostini page 70)

cook's tip

You will find many good-quality commercial compotes or chutneys at the market today, especially those made

with fruits such as mango or apple. Either would be a good substitution in this recipe. Other cheeses such as Jarlsberg, mild goat cheese, or manchego would make a nice addition to this arrangement.

cook's tip

Dips are ideal for using up fresh
vegetables that you have on hand.
For example, cut carrots and
zucchini (courgettes) crosswise
into think slices or spears and
serve with the white bean dip
alongside the pita.

white bean dip with pita

1 Make the dip
Preheat the oven to 300°F (150°C). In a small frying pan over medium-low heat, warm 1 tablespoon of the oil. Add the prosciutto, if using, and the fresh sage and cook, stirring occasionally, until crisp and golden, about 4 minutes. Add the garlic, stir, and remove from the heat. In a food processor, combine the beans and shallot and process until smooth. Transfer to a bowl and stir in the sautéed sage mixture, lemon juice, 1 tablespoon of the olive oil, ¼ teaspoon salt, and pepper to taste. Set aside for the flavors to come together.

2 Warm the pita
Place the pita quarters on a baking sheet. Brush both sides lightly with the remaining 2 tablespoons olive oil. Sprinkle evenly with the dried sage and heat in the oven until crisp and warmed through, about 10 minutes. Place the toasted pita on a small platter and serve alongside the bowl of bean dip.

Olive oil, 4 tablespoons (2 fl oz/60 ml)

Prosciutto, 1 oz (30 g), finely chopped (optional)

Fresh sage leaves, 4–6, finely chopped

Garlic, 1 clove, very finely chopped

Cannellini beans, 1 can (15½ oz/485 g), rinsed and drained

Shallot, 1, very finely chopped

Lemon juice, 2 teaspoons

Salt and freshly ground pepper

Pita bread, 6 rounds, each cut into quarters

Dried sage, 1 teaspoon

MAKES ABOUT 2 CUPS (16 OZ/500 G)

ricotta, fig & prosciutto bruschetta

French or sourdough baguette, 24 slices, each about ½ inch (12 mm) thick

Olive oil, 2 tablespoons

Fig jam or preserves, 1 cup (10 oz/315 g)

Whole-milk ricotta cheese, 1¼ cups (10 oz/315 g)

Prosciutto, 6 thin slices, each cut into 4 pieces

Freshly ground pepper

MAKES ABOUT 24 BRUSCHETTA

1 Toast the bread
Prehcat the oven to 350°F (180°C). Arrange the baguette slices on a baking sheet and brush lightly with the olive oil. Bake until golden, 10–15 minutes. Transfer to a platter.

2 Assemble the bruschetta
Spread each slice with a generous teaspoon of the fig jam. Top with a dollop of the ricotta and a piece of prosciutto. Season with pepper and serve at once.

cook's tip

Some types of fig preserves or
jam use whole figs, making it too
chunky to spread. To solve this
problem, place in a food processor
and pulse once or twice until the
figs are broken down and the
jam is spreadable.

cook's tip

Choose from the astounding
array of different sea salts that
are now available—from delicate
marine algae salt to orange
Hawaiian salt harvested from
lava beds in the sea. For the
ultimate experience, seek out
hand-harvested Fleur de Sel.

radishes with butter & sea salt

1 Whip the butter and prepare the radishes
Place the butter in a small bowl. Using a fork, whip the butter until light and fluffy and set aside. Trim the stems and root ends from the radishes.

2 Assemble the platter
Transfer the butter to a ramekin or a small serving bowl for dipping or spreading and place alongside the radishes on a platter or serving tray. Place a mound of about 2–3 tablespoons sea salt on the platter or in a small bowl for sprinkling and serve.

Unsalted butter, ½ cup (4 oz/125 g), at room temperature

Radishes, 3–4 bunches, about 32, chilled

Sea salt

MAKES ABOUT
32 SMALL BITES

21

salmon & herbed cheese pinwheels

Smoked salmon, 6 oz (185 g), thinly sliced

Cream cheese, ¼ lb (125 g), at room temperature

Fresh basil, 1 teaspoon roughly chopped

Fresh chives, 2 teaspoons roughly snipped

Ground white pepper

Flour tortillas, 4, each about 8 inches (20 cm) in diameter

MAKES ABOUT
24 PINWHEELS

1 Mix the filling
Set aside three-fourths of the largest slices of smoked salmon. Place the remaining slices in a food processor with the cream cheese, basil, chives, and ¼ teaspoon pepper. Pulse to blend.

2 Assemble the pinwheels
Spread each tortilla with one-fourth of the cream cheese mixture. Divide the reserved slices of salmon between 4 tortillas, placing the salmon horizontally across the center of each tortilla. Starting from the bottom, roll each tortilla firmly. Trim the ends and cut each rolled tortilla into 6 slices. Arrange the pinwheels on a platter, cut side up, and serve.

cook's tip

Once completely cool, the
nuts may be stored in an airtight
container or a plastic freezer
bag at room temperature for up
to 2 days. Or, refrigerate them
for up to two weeks. Remember
to bring the nuts to room
temperature before serving.

spiced roasted nuts

1 Prepare the seasonings

Preheat the oven to 350°F (180°C). Line a rimmed baking sheet with aluminum foil. In a large saucepan over medium heat, combine the butter, curry powder, 2 teaspoons salt, cinnamon, cumin, cayenne, and brown sugar. Cook, stirring occasionally, just until the butter is melted and the flavors are released, 2–3 minutes.

2 Roast the nuts

Using a spatula, add the nuts to the spice mixture and toss until evenly coated. Spread the nuts on the prepared baking sheet in a single layer. Bake until deep golden brown, about 15 minutes. Slide the foil and nuts onto a wire rack and let cool completely before serving.

Unsalted butter,
4 tablespoons (2 oz/60 g)

Curry powder, 1 tablespoon

Salt

Ground cinnamon,
½ teaspoon

Ground cumin, ½ teaspoon

Cayenne pepper, 1 teaspoon

Brown sugar, 1 tablespoon
packed

Pecans or mixed nuts, 1 lb
(500 g)

MAKES ABOUT 4 CUPS
(1 LB/500 G)

caprese
skewers

Fresh mozzarella balls, 12, halved

Cherry tomatoes, 12, halved lengthwise

Fresh basil leaves, 12 large, torn in half

Olive oil for drizzling

Salt and freshly ground pepper

MAKES ABOUT
24 SKEWERS

1 Assemble the skewers

Thread 1 tomato half, 1 mozzarella ball half, and 1 basil leaf half on a wooden toothpick. Repeat to make the remaining skewers. Arrange on a platter and drizzle with the olive oil. Season generously with salt and pepper and serve. (The skewers may be covered and refrigerated for up to 2 hours; serve chilled or at room temperature.)

cook's tip

If you cannot find *bocconcini* (small mozzarella balls) at your local market, you can use whole fresh mozzarella. Using a sharp chef's knife, cut the mozzarella into ½-inch (12-mm) slices and cut each slice into ½-inch cubes.

thai
lettuce cups

cook's tip

Lemongrass is available
in many markets, but if you
can't find it, substitute
1 tablespoon lemon juice
and 2 teaspoons grated

lemon zest. Add the
juice and zest to the pork
mixture in Step 2.

1 Cook the pork and sausage

In a frying pan over medium-low heat, cook the pork
and sausage, stirring to break the meat apart, until no trace
of pink remains, about 8 minutes. Using a slotted spoon,
transfer to a double layer of paper towels and let cool for
5 minutes. Crumble into small bits.

2 Assemble the lettuce cups

In a bowl, combine the pork mixture, green onions,
bell pepper, lemongrass, mint, sesame oil, soy sauce, fish
sauce, and sesame seeds. Place about 2 tablespoons of the
pork mixture in the center of each lettuce leaf. Arrange the
cups on a platter, and serve.

Ground (minced) pork,
¾ lb (375 g)

**Sweet or hot pork
sausage,** ¾ lb (375 g),
casings removed

Green (spring) onions,
4, white and pale green parts
only, thinly sliced

**Red bell pepper
(capsicum),** ½, seeded and
finely chopped

Lemongrass, 1 stalk, bulb
part only, trimmed and minced

Fresh mint, 1 teaspoon finely
chopped

Asian sesame oil,
2 teaspoons

Soy sauce, 2 teaspoons

Asian fish sauce,
2 teaspoons

Sesame seeds, 2 teaspoons

Butter (Boston) lettuce,
2 or 3 heads, separated into
about 22 leaves

MAKES ABOUT
22 LETTUCE CUPS

turkey & manchego sandwiches

French or sourdough baguette, 24 slices, each about ½ inch (12 mm) thick

Mayonnaise, ½ cup (4 fl oz/ 125 ml)

Whole-grain mustard, ⅓ cup (3 oz/90 g)

Smoked turkey, 5 oz (155 g), thinly sliced

Manchego or aged pecorino cheese, 5 oz (155 g), thinly sliced

Baby arugula (rocket) or spinach leaves, 2 cups (2 oz/60 g)

MAKES 12 SANDWICHES

1 Assemble the sandwiches

Spread each baguette slice with about 1 teaspoon mayonnaise and spread half of the slices with the mustard. Divide the turkey, cheese, and arugula among the slices without the mustard, and top with the remaining baguette slices. Arrange on a platter, and serve.

cook's tip

Many other ingredients will work equally well for these sandwiches. Experiment with your favorite cured meats and cheeses, or make a smoked salmon and cream cheese sandwich with crisp greens.

cook's tip

Using smoked paprika gives the
fried garbanzos a complex,
smoky flavor. Look for this variety
in stores specializing in Hispanic
ingredients. The best varieties are
from Spain, where it is known
as *pimentón*. If it is unavailable,
substitute Hungarian hot paprika.

fried
garbanzos

1 Dry the garbanzo beans and heat the oil

Preheat the oven to 200°F (95°C). Arrange a double layer of paper towels on a rimmed baking sheet and place in the oven. On another layer of paper towels, spread the drained garbanzo beans and gently roll to dry them. Set a heavy frying pan over high heat. Add equal amounts of olive oil and canola oil to reach about ¾ inch (2 cm) up the sides of the pan. Heat the oil until it reaches 350°F (180°C) on a deep-frying thermometer.

2 Cook the garbanzo beans

Add half of the garbanzo beans to the hot oil and fry, stirring occasionally, until golden and slightly puffed, 2–3 minutes. Adjust the heat to maintain an oil temperature of about 350°F (180°C). Using a slotted spoon, transfer the beans to the paper towel–lined sheet, season with salt and pepper, and keep warm in the oven. Repeat the process with the remaining garbanzo beans. Add the second batch of garbanzo beans to the first, toss with the paprika, and serve.

Garbanzo beans (chickpeas), 2 cans (15⅕ oz/485 g each), rinsed and drained

Olive oil for frying

Canola oil for frying

Coarse salt and freshly ground pepper

Smoked paprika, ½ teaspoon

MAKES ABOUT 2 CUPS (12 OZ/370 G)

crab salad
with endive

Fennel bulb, ½, trimmed, quartered lengthwise, and finely chopped

Fresh lump crabmeat, ½ lb (250 g), picked over for shell fragments

Shallot, 1, finely chopped

Fresh chives, 1 tablespoon finely snipped, plus more for garnish

Fresh flat-leaf (Italian) parsley, 1 tablespoon finely chopped

Mayonnaise, 2 tablespoons

Crème fraîche or sour cream, 1 tablespoon

Juice from 1 lemon

Salt and ground white pepper

Belgian endive (chicory/ witloof), 6 large heads

MAKES 24 PIECES

1 **Prepare the crab salad**
In a bowl, stir together the fennel, crabmeat, shallot, 1 tablespoon chives, parsley, mayonnaise, crème fraîche, lemon juice, ¼ teaspoon salt, and ¼ teaspoon pepper. Taste and adjust the seasonings if necessary.

2 **Assemble the salad**
Trim the root ends from the endive heads and separate into spears. Arrange 24 of the largest spears on a platter. Spoon a generous amount of crab salad onto the wide end of each spear, garnish with the remaining chives, and serve.

cook's tip

You can change the flavor of this quesadilla by substituting a cured sausage or peppered salami for the chorizo. If using a cured pork product, omit the initial cooking and simply cut it into small dice.

chorizo & cheese quesadillas

1 Fry the sausage

In a large frying pan over medium heat, cook the chorizo, stirring to break it apart, until browned, about 6 minutes. Using a slotted spoon, transfer to a paper towel–lined plate and let cool for 5 minutes. Using your hands, crumble into small bits. In a bowl, toss together the Jack and cheddar cheeses, green onions, and cooked chorizo.

2 Cook the quesadillas

Wipe out the chorizo pan with paper towels, add 1 teaspoon canola oil, and set over medium-low heat. Working in batches, place one tortilla in the pan and scatter one-quarter of the cheese-chorizo mixture evenly over the tortilla, leaving a ½-inch (12-mm) border uncovered. Top with a second tortilla. Cook, pressing down with a spatula occasionally, until golden brown on the first side, about 2 minutes. Using a large spatula, carefully turn the quesadilla and cook until golden on the second side and the cheese has melted, about 1 minute longer. Repeat this process to make 4 quesadillas total. Cut each quesadilla into wedges and arrange on a platter. Sprinkle with *queso fresco* and cilantro and serve.

Fresh chorizo sausage, ¼ lb (125 g), casings removed

Jalapeño Jack cheese, 1⅓ cups (5 oz/155 g) coarsely grated

White cheddar cheese, 1⅓ cups (5 oz/155 g) coarsely grated

Green (spring) onions, 4, white and pale green parts only, very thinly sliced

Canola oil for frying

Flour tortillas, 8, each about 8 inches (20 cm) in diameter

Queso fresco, 1 cup (5 oz/ 155 g) crumbled

Fresh cilantro (fresh coriander), ¼ cup (⅓ oz/ 10 g) coarsely chopped

MAKES ABOUT
24 WEDGES

37

goat cheese stuffed tomatoes

Fresh goat cheese, ¼ lb (125 g), at room temperature

Cream cheese, 3 oz (90 g), at room temperature

Sour cream, 2 tablespoons

Cherry tomatoes, 2½ cups (16 oz/400 g), about 40, stem ends trimmed

Fresh chives, 2 tablespoons finely snipped

MAKES ABOUT 40 TOMATOES

1 Mix the filling
In a food processor, combine the goat cheese, cream cheese, and sour cream. Process until smooth, scraping down the sides if necessary.

2 Stuff the tomatoes
Using the small end of a melon baller, carefully scoop out the seeds and core from each tomato. Arrange the tomatoes cut side up on a cutting board. Using 2 small spoons, place about 1 teaspoon of the goat cheese filling in each tomato, mounding it slightly. Tranfer to a platter, sprinkle with the chives, and serve.

cook's tip

To make the stuffed tomatoes in advance, prepare the recipe through Step 1. Hollow out the tomatoes and arrange, cut side down on a paper towel–lined baking sheet. Cover with plastic wrap and refrigerate along with the goat cheese filling for up to 3 hours. Fill the tomatoes before serving.

cook's tip

Commonly, peaches are peeled
by blanching them and removing
the skin with your fingers. If you
don't have the time to blanch the
peaches; halve them lengthwise,
and, using a vegetable peeler
or a sharp paring knife, carefully
remove the skin in long strips.

peaches with prosciutto & mint

1 **Cut the peaches and prosciutto**
Halve each peach and remove the pit. Cut each peach half into 4 equal wedges. Cut each prosciutto slice lengthwise into 3 strips.

2 **Assemble the appetizers**
Place a mint leaf on each peach wedge and wrap with a strip of the prosciutto. If desired, secure with a toothpick. Transfer to a platter and serve.

Yellow or white peaches, 3, peeled if desired

Prosciutto, 8 thin slices

Fresh mint leaves, 24

MAKES 24 PIECES

30 minutes
start to finish

crostini with steak & horseradish cream

Flank steak, 1 ½ lb (750 g), trimmed of excess fat

Olive oil, 3 tablespoons

Salt and freshly ground pepper

Prepared horseradish, 2 tablespoons

Sour cream, 3 tablespoons

French or sourdough baguette, cut into slices ½ inch (12 mm) thick

Paprika for garnish

MAKES ABOUT
28 CROSTINI

1 Season the steak
Preheat the oven to 350°F (180°C). Place a rack in a roasting pan. Brush both sides of the steak with 1 tablespoon of the oil. Season generously with salt and pepper. Place on the rack and let stand at room temperature. In a small bowl, whisk together the horseradish and sour cream.

2 Make the crostini
Arrange the baguette slices on a baking sheet and brush lightly with the remaining olive oil. Season with salt and pepper. Bake until golden, 10–15 minutes. Transfer to a platter.

3 Cook the steak
Preheat the broiler (grill). Broil (grill) the steak until firm but still quite pink in the center, about 6 minutes per side. Let rest for 5 minutes. Cut the steak with the grain into slices about 2 inches (5 cm) thick, then thinly cut the slices crosswise across the grain. Arrange 1 or 2 slices on each crostini, top with a dollop of the horseradish cream, and sprinkle with paprika. Transfer to a platter and serve at room temperature.

cook's tip

Instead of horseradish cream serve these steak crostini topped with a spicy, garlicky aioli. To prepare a quick aioli, mix 1 teaspoon minced garlic and ½ teaspoon paprika into ½ cup (4 fl oz/25 ml) good-quality mayonnaise, and season to taste with salt.

cook's tip

Instead of sweet potato chips, use 8-inch (20-cm) corn tortillas, cut into wedges, as a substitute. Stack tortillas, and, using a sharp knife, cut the stack in half. Then cut each half into 8 wedges and continue to cook according to Step 1. Or, you can substitute your favorite purchased chips.

guacamole & sweet potato chips

1 Make the sweet potato chips

Preheat the oven to 500°F (260°C). Lightly brush 2 baking sheets with olive oil. Arrange the sweet potato slices in a single layer on the prepared sheets and drizzle with the remaining olive oil. Bake until the slices are golden and crisp, about 10 minutes. Turn the slices, rotate the pans, and cook until golden and crisp on the second side, about 10 minutes longer. Transfer to paper towels to drain. Season with salt and let stand at room temperature for 5 minutes. Transfer to a platter.

2 Prepare the guacamole

Meanwhile, scoop the flesh from the avocado halves and add to a bowl. Mash with a fork. Add the onion, cilantro, chile, lime juice, and ½ teaspoon salt. Stir to combine. Garnish with the shallot and cilantro leaves and serve in a bowl alongside the chips.

Olive oil, 2 tablespoons

Sweet potatoes, 1 lb (500 g), peeled, halved lengthwise, and cut crosswise into very thin slices

Salt

Avocados, 2, halved and pitted

White onion, 2 tablespoons very finely chopped

Fresh cilantro (fresh coriander), ¼ cup (⅓ oz/ 10 g) finely chopped

Serrano chile, ½ small, seeded and very finely chopped

Juice of 1 lime

Shallot, 2 tablespoons finely chopped

Fresh cilantro (fresh coriander) leaves, ¼ cup (¼ oz/7 g)

MAKES ABOUT
2 CUPS (16 OZ/500 G)
GUACAMOLE

47

spring rolls with lime-cilantro sauce

Medium shrimp (prawns), 1 lb (500 g), about 24, peeled, deveined, and cooked

Green onions, 6, white and pale green parts only, thinly sliced

Fresh cilantro (fresh coriander), 3 tablespoons chopped

Lime juice, ½ cup (4 fl oz/ 125 ml)

Brown sugar, 2 tablespoons packed

Asian fish sauce, 3 tablespoons

Rice vinegar, 1 tablespoon

Garlic, 1 clove, minced

Rice paper rounds, 12

Cucumber, 1, peeled, halved lengthwise, seeded, and thinly sliced

Dried vermicelli or rice stick noodles, 4 oz (125 g), soaked in hot water for 15 minutes and drained

MAKES 12 SPRING ROLLS

1 Prepare the filling and sauce
In a bowl, stir together the shrimp, green onions, and 2 tablespoons of the cilantro. In another bowl, whisk together the lime juice, brown sugar, fish sauce, vinegar, garlic, and remaining 1 tablespoon cilantro until the sugar dissolves. Let stand for 5 minutes.

2 Assemble the rolls
Have ready a large, shallow bowl of warm water and a damp kitchen towel. Immerse each rice paper round in the water for 2 or 3 seconds. Spread it on the towel; it will become pliable within a few seconds. Divide the shrimp mixture horizontally near the bottom of the rice paper. Top with some of the cucumber slices and noodles. Lift the bottom edge of the rice paper over the filling, compacting it gently but firmly. Fold in the sides and roll the rice paper toward the top edge, again compacting gently. Using a sharp knife, cut each roll in half on the diagonal. Arrange on a platter and serve with the dipping sauce.

cook's tip

If desired, you may purchase
fresh mango salsa to use in place
of the pineapple salsa. The fresh
pineapple salsa may be prepared
up to 4 hours before serving
and refrigerated. If it is stored for
longer, the pineapple may
develop a mushy texture.

grilled pork with pineapple salsa

1 Marinate the pork

Place 22 bamboo skewers in water to soak for 20 minutes. Prepare a gas or charcoal grill for direct grilling over medium heat. Alternatively, preheat the broiler (griller). In a large bowl, stir together the pork, olive oil, and garlic. Season generously with salt and pepper and toss to combine. Let stand for 15 minutes.

2 Marinate the pork

Meanwhile, in a glass or ceramic bowl, stir together the pineapple, onion, bell pepper, mint, cilantro, and ¼ teaspoon salt. Set aside while you cook the pork.

3 Cook the pork

Thread 3 cubes of pork onto each skewer, pushing them snugly together. Place the skewers on the grill rack and cook, turning the skewers halfway through the cooking time, until firm and just lightly browned, about 6 minutes. Alternatively, arrange the skewers on a broiler pan and broil (grill), turning them halfway through the cooking time, for about 6 minutes. Transfer the skewers to a platter and serve alongside the salsa.

Boneless pork loin,
1 lb (500 g), cut into ¾-inch (2-cm) cubes

Olive oil, 2 tablespoons

Garlic, 2 cloves, minced

Salt and freshly ground pepper

Pineapple, 1½ cups (9 oz/280g) finely chopped

Red onion, ½ , finely chopped

Large red bell pepper (capsicum), ½, finely chopped

Fresh mint leaves, 6, minced

Fresh cilantro (fresh coriander), 2 teaspoons minced

MAKES ABOUT
22 SKEWERS

51

shrimp skewers
with basil oil

Fresh basil leaves, ½ cup
(½ oz/15 g)

Extra-virgin olive oil, ⅔ cup
(5 fl oz/160 ml)

Large shrimp (prawns),
1 ½ pounds (750 g), peeled
and deveined

**Salt and freshly ground
pepper**

MAKES ABOUT
28 SKEWERS

1 **Make the basil oil**
Bring a small saucepan of water to a boil. Add the basil, stir once to immerse, and cook for 45 seconds. Drain in a colander and rinse under cold running water to stop the cooking. Squeeze the basil leaves in a paper towel to extract as much water as possible. In a mini–food processor, combine the basil and the olive oil. Pulse until blended, scraping down the sides of the container.

2 **Cook the shrimp**
Preheat the broiler (grill). Place a rack on a baking sheet. Thread 2 shrimp on each skewer, running it through both the tail and the head of each shrimp. Place on the rack. Brush the shrimp with some of the basil oil and season lightly with salt and pepper. Broil (grill) the shrimp, without turning, until firm and pink, about 4 minutes. Transfer to a platter, drizzle with a little more basil oil, and serve.

cook's tip

This technique can be adapted for woodier herbs such as rosemary. In a small saucepan, bring 1 cup (8 fl oz/250 ml) of good-quality olive oil and 2 sprigs of rosemary to a boil. Remove from the heat and let stand for 15 minutes. Remove the rosemary before using. Pair with grilled lamb, chicken, or fish.

cook's tip

Use a gentle touch when shaping the meatballs. This prevents the meat from compacting and absorbing warmth from your hands,

ensuring light and tender results. Keep a bowl of water nearby and wet your hands occasionally to form smooth meatballs. The uncooked meatballs may be refrigerated for up to 4 hours. Remove them 15 minutes before cooking. They can also be frozen for up to 1 month. Thaw before cooking.

lamb meatballs
with cilantro raita

1 Shape the meatballs

Preheat the broiler (grill). Lightly oil a rimmed baking sheet. In a frying pan over medium-low heat, warm the olive oil. Add the onion and cook, stirring occasionally, until soft, about 5 minutes. Transfer the onion to a large bowl and add the lamb, eggs, parsley, bread crumbs, cumin, three-fourths of the garlic, 1 teaspoon salt, and ½ teaspoon pepper. Using your hands, combine the ingredients. Form the mixture into walnut-sized balls, rolling them lightly between your palms. Place on the prepared baking sheet.

2 Cook the meatballs

Broil (grill) the meatballs, turning once, until brown and crispy, 8–10 minutes.

3 Make the raita

Meanwhile, in a small bowl, whisk together the yogurt, cilantro, remaining garlic, and ¼ teaspoon salt. Secure each meatball with a toothpick, place on a platter, and serve alongside the raita.

Olive oil, 2 tablespoons

Yellow onion, 1 small, minced

Ground (minced) lamb, 1 lb (500 g)

Eggs, 2, lightly beaten

Fresh, flat-leaf (Italian) parsley, ½ cup (¾ oz/20 g), minced

Fine dried bread crumbs, 2 tablespoons

Ground cumin, 1 teaspoon

Garlic, 4 large cloves, minced

Salt and freshly ground pepper

Plain yogurt, 1 cup (8 oz/250 g)

Fresh cilantro (fresh coriander), 2 tablespoons finely chopped

MAKES ABOUT
42 MEATBALLS

artichokes with lemon aioli

Lemon, 1

Baby artichokes, 14

Olive oil, ¼ cup (2 fl oz/ 60 ml)

Salt and freshly ground pepper

Mayonnaise, ⅔ cup (5 fl oz/160 ml)

Garlic, 1 clove, minced

MAKES 28 PIECES

1 **Trim the artichokes**
Grate 1 teaspoon zest from the lemon and set aside. Halve the lemon, reserving one half and squeezing 2 teaspoons juice from the other. Reserve the juice and both lemon halves. Snap off the tough outer leaves from each artichoke and trim the spiny tops and the stem. Remove any fibrous portions around the base. Halve the artichokes. As you work, rub all the cut areas with the reserved lemon half.

2 **Cook the artichokes**
Bring a large pot of lightly salted water to a boil. Add the two lemon halves and the artichokes, reduce the heat to medium, and simmer until the bases are tender, about 6 minutes. Drain in a colander and rinse under cold running water to stop the cooking. Discard the lemon halves. Preheat a grill pan over medium heat. In a bowl, toss the artichoke halves with the olive oil until evenly coated. Season with salt and pepper and toss again. Place the artichokes in the pan and cook, turning occasionally, until they are crisp and grill marks appear, about 10 minutes.

3 **Make the aioli**
Meanwhile, in a bowl, whisk together the mayonnaise, garlic, and reserved lemon zest and juice. Transfer the artichokes to a platter and serve with the aioli.

cook's tip

Make a quick and spicy lemon dipping sauce to accompany the fritto misto. Mix together ½ cup (4 fl oz/125 ml) of mayonnaise, 1 tablespoon lemon juice, and ½ teaspoon of cayenne pepper and season to taste with salt and freshly ground black pepper.

fritto misto

1 Heat the oil

Preheat the oven to 250°F (120°C). Line a baking sheet with paper towels, set a rack on the towels, and place in the oven. Fill a large, heavy saucepan with peanut oil to a depth of about 2 inches (5 cm). Place over high heat and heat the oil until it reaches 400°F (200°C) on a deep-frying thermometer.

2 Cook the seafood

In a large shallow bowl, whisk together the flour, 1 teaspoon salt, and 1 teaspoon pepper. Working in small batches, toss the squid and shrimp in the flour mixture, coating them evenly, and shake off any excess. Using a wire skimmer, lower the seafood into the hot oil. Fry, turning once, until golden, 3–4 minutes. Using the skimmer, remove the seafood from the oil, place on the prepared baking sheet and transfer to the warm oven. Let the oil return to 400°F before cooking another batch. Transfer the seafood to a platter, garnish with the lemon slices, and serve.

Peanut oil for frying

Cake (soft-wheat) flour,
2 cups (8 oz/250 g)

Salt and freshly ground pepper

Squid bodies and tentacles, ¾ lb (375 g), bodies cut crosswise into rings

Medium shrimp (prawns),
¾ lb (375 g), peeled and deveined, tails intact

Lemon, 1, ends trimmed and very thinly sliced

MAKES ABOUT
40 PIECES

potato pancakes with smoked salmon

Small baking potatoes, 1¼ lb (625 g), peeled

Flour, ½ cup (2½ oz/75 g)

Yellow onion, ½ small, grated

Salt and ground white pepper

Egg, 1, lightly beaten

Olive oil, 1 tablespoon

Unsalted butter, 1 tablespoon, melted

Crème fraîche or sour cream, 1 cup (8 oz/250 g)

Smoked salmon, 6 oz (185 g), cut into slivers

Fresh chives, 1 tablespoon finely snipped

MAKES ABOUT 24 PANCAKES

1 Form the pancakes

Bring a pan of lightly salted water to a boil. Add the potatoes and cook until almost tender, about 10 minutes. Drain in a colander and rinse under cold running water to stop the cooking. Drain well and pat dry with paper towels. Using the largest holes of a box grater-shredder, grate the potatoes into a large bowl. Add the flour, onion, ½ teaspoon salt, and ¼ teaspoon pepper and combine well with a fork. Stir in the egg. With lightly floured hands, form the mixture into walnut-sized balls, rolling them between your palms, then flatten into patties.

2 Cook the pancakes

In a small bowl, combine the olive oil and butter. Place a large frying pan over medium heat and brush generously with the butter mixture. Working in batches, cook the pancakes until golden and crisp, 4–5 minutes per side. Transfer to a paper towel–lined plate. Top each pancake with a dollop of the crème fraîche and a few slivers of salmon. Arrange on a serving platter, sprinkle with the chives, and serve.

cook's tip

After the pancakes are cooked,
let them rest briefly on a paper
towel–lined plate to absorb any
excess oil before topping and
serving. They may also be kept
warm in a 200°F (95°C) oven,
although they may lose some
of their crispness.

cook's tip

Using pitted dates speeds
the preparation. If they are not
available, use a small, sharp
knife to make a slit along the side
of each date and pull out the pit.
The bacon will help seal the
date so the cheese does not leak
out, and it will also cover the
ragged edges.

roasted dates with parmesan & bacon

1 Prepare the filling
Preheat the oven to 400°F (200°C) and place a baking sheet in the oven to heat. In a small bowl, combine the Parmesan and cream cheese and mix until smooth.

2 Fill the dates
Slice each date along one side to make a pocket and insert 1–2 teaspoons of the cheese filling. Wrap a piece of bacon around each stuffed date. The bacon should cover the opening in the date and overlap slightly. Secure the dates with small wooden skewers or toothpicks. (The dates may be refrigerated overnight; return to room temperature for about 15 minutes before roasting.)

3 Cook the dates
Using tongs, place the dates on the hot baking sheet. Roast until the bacon is crisp, 15–20 minutes. Transfer to a platter and serve at once.

Parmesan cheese, ¼ lb (125 g), coarsely grated

Cream cheese, 2 tablespoons, at room temperature

Pitted dates, preferably Medjool, 18

Lean bacon, 6 slices, each cut crosswise into 3 pieces

MAKES 18 DATES

63

tamarind-glazed chicken wings

Chicken wings or drumettes, 24, patted dry

Salt and freshly ground pepper

Canola oil, ¼ cup (2 fl oz/ 60 ml)

Garlic, 4 large cloves, minced

Tamarind paste or concentrate, 3 tablespoons

Red wine vinegar, 3 tablespoons

Honey, 3 tablespoons

Green (spring) onions, 4, white and pale green parts only, minced

MAKES 24 WINGS

1 **Glaze the chicken**
In a large glass or ceramic bowl, toss the chicken with ¾ teaspoon salt and ¼ teaspoon pepper. In a large frying pan over medium-low heat, warm the oil. Cook the garlic, stirring constantly, until translucent, about 2 minutes. Remove from the heat, add the tamarind paste and vinegar, and whisk until smooth. Set aside ¼ cup (2 fl oz/60 ml) of the glaze for basting. Add the chicken to the frying pan with the remaining glaze and toss to coat.

2 **Cook the chicken**
Preheat the oven to 400°F (200°C). Transfer the chicken to a baking sheet, discarding the marinade in the pan. Roast, turning occasionally, for 10 minutes. Stir the honey into the reserved glaze. Continue to roast, basting the chicken and turning them occasionally, until firm and golden, about 15 minutes longer. Transfer to a platter, garnish with the green onions, and serve.

cook's tip

For a stronger, more concentrated flavor, place the wings in a resealable freezer bag or in a tightly covered dish and marinate overnight. Bring to room temperature before roasting.

cook's tip

For the best results, use nonstick mini muffin pans, so the popovers can be easily freed from the cups. If the popovers happen to get stuck, gently pry them out with a small icing spatula or offset spatula, as a paring knife may scratch the pan.

gruyère-chive popovers

1 Make the batter

Preheat the oven to 450°F (230°C). Generously oil 2 mini muffin pans. In a large bowl, whisk together the flour, ½ teaspoon salt, ¼ teaspoon pepper, and chives. In a large measuring pitcher, whisk together the milk, eggs, and butter. Pour the wet ingredients over the dry ingredients and whisk together until just combined (don't worry if some lumps remain).

2 Bake the popovers

Fill the prepared muffin cups to within about ¼ inch (6 mm) of the rims. Place a scant teaspoon grated cheese in the center of each filled cup. Bake, without opening the oven door, for 10 minutes. Reduce the oven temperature to 350°F (180°C) and bake until the popovers are brown, crusty, and fully puffed, 8–10 minutes longer. Transfer to a platter and serve warm.

Canola oil for greasing

Flour, 1 cup (5 oz/155 g)

Salt and freshly ground pepper

Fresh chives, 1 tablespoon finely snipped

Milk, 1¼ cups (10 fl oz/ 310 ml), at room temperature

Eggs, 2, at room temperature

Unsalted butter, 1 tablespoon, melted

Gruyère cheese, 3 oz (90 g), coarsely grated

MAKES 24 POPOVERS

scallops with mango & avocado

Bay scallops or sea scallops, 1¼ lb (625 g), side muscles removed

Canola oil, 1–2 tablespoons

Juice from 7 or 8 limes (1¼ cups/10 fl oz/310 ml)

Fresh cilantro (fresh cilantro), 1½ tablespoons finely chopped

Salt and freshly ground pepper

Red pepper flakes, ¾ teaspoon

Hot sauce such as tabasco to taste

Mango, 1, peeled, pitted, and cut into small cubes

Avocado, 1, pitted, peeled, and cut into small cubes

Olive oil for drizzling

MAKES ABOUT
4 CUPS

1 Cook the scallops

If using large sea scallops, cut the scallops in half hortizontally. In a large frying pan over medium-high heat, warm 1 tablespoon of the canola oil until hot but not smoking. Working in batches so the pan is not crowded, sear the scallops on each side for 1–2 minutes, adding more oil if necessary. Transfer the seared scallops to a plate.

2 Marinate the scallops

In a glass or ceramic bowl, combine the lime juice, cilantro, 2 teaspoons salt, pepper flakes, and hot sauce. Add the scallops and toss. Gently stir in the mango and avocado. Spoon into martini glasses. Drizzle with olive oil and serve.

cook's tip

Make a double batch of eggplant
pesto and serve on crostini—you
will have two appetizers in one.
To make the crostini, preheat the
oven to 350°F (180°C). Arrange
the baguette slices on a baking
sheet and brush lightly with
the olive oil. Season with salt and
pepper. Bake until golden,
10–15 minutes.

polenta with eggplant pesto

1 Make the eggplant pesto
Preheat the oven to 400°F (200°C). Toss the eggplant with the 2 tablespoons olive oil. Season generously with salt. Place in a baking pan skin side down and bake until soft and tender, about 20 minutes. Let cool slightly. In a food processor or blender, combine the eggplant, garlic, pine nuts, and 1/2 teaspoon salt. Pulse until smooth. Add the basil and 1/3 cup olive oil, and pulse until smooth, scraping down the sides of the container. Transfer to a bowl and fold in the cheese.

2 Cook the polenta
Meanwhile, line a baking sheet with paper towels. While the eggplant is baking, in a large frying pan over medium heat, warm the canola oil. Season the polenta slices on both sides with salt and pepper. Add 10 slices to the pan and cook, turning once, until golden brown, about 4 minutes per side. Transfer to the baking sheet and cook the remaining polenta slices. Arrange the slices on a platter, top with a generous spoonful of the eggplant pesto, sprinkle with pepper, and serve.

Eggplant, 1 large (about 1 1/4 lb/625 g), peeled, quartered lengthwise, and cut into 2-inch (5-cm) pieces

Olive oil, 2 tablespoons, plus 1/3 cup (3 fl oz/80 ml)

Salt and freshly ground pepper

Garlic, 2 cloves, finely chopped

Pine nuts, 2 tablespoons

Fresh basil leaves, 1 cup (1 oz/30 g)

Parmesan cheese, 1/2 cup (2 oz/60 g) grated

Canola oil, 2 tablespoons

Precooked polenta, 2 tubes (about 17 oz/530 g each), ends trimmed and cut into 20 slices total

MAKES 20 ROUNDS

tomatillo gazpacho

Fresh tomatillos, 1 lb (500 g), husked, rinsed, and coarsely chopped

White grape juice, 1 cup (8 fl oz/250 ml)

Green bell pepper (capsicum), 1, seeded and coarsely chopped

Green (spring) onions, 5, white and pale green parts only, sliced

Jalapeño chile, 1, seeded and coarsely chopped

Lime juice, 1–2 tablespoons

Fresh cilantro (fresh coriander) leaves, 2 tablespoons

Salt and freshly ground pepper

Plain yogurt, ¼ cup (2 oz/60 g) for garnish

MAKES 24 SHOTS

1 Purée the vegetables
In a blender or food processor, combine the tomatillos, grape juice, bell pepper, green onions, jalapeño, 1½ tablespoons of the lime juice, the cilantro, 1 teaspoon salt, and ½ teaspoon pepper. Pulse until the mixture is smooth, scraping down the sides of the container, 2–3 minutes.

2 Finish the soup
Transfer to a large bowl and refrigerate for 15 minutes. Stir well to combine. Taste and adjust the seasonings with salt, pepper, and lime juice. Pour into chilled shot glasses, garnish with the yogurt, and serve.

cook's tip

For a very cold gazpacho, refrigerate for 1–2 hours before serving. The soup will separate; using a whisk, stir vigorously just before serving to incorporate the ingredients.

cook's tip

Chopped fresh dill may
be substituted for the
tarragon, and diced Belgian
endive (chicory/witloof)
for the fennel. The resulting
salad will have a more
Scandinavian flavor than
this Mediterranean appetizer.

lemon chicken
salad on crostini

1 **Make the crostini**
Preheat the oven to 350°F (180°C). Arrange the baguette slices on a baking sheet and brush lightly with the olive oil. Season with salt and pepper. Bake until golden, 10–15 minutes. Transfer to a platter.

2 **Cook the chicken**
Meanwhile, grate ½ teaspoon zest from the lemon. Halve the lemon and squeeze 1 teaspoon juice. Set the zest and juice aside. Season both sides of the chicken breasts with salt and pepper. In a large frying pan over medium heat, warm the canola oil. Add the chicken and cook until golden brown and opaque, 4–5 minutes per side. Transfer to a cutting board and let stand for 5 minutes.

3 **Prepare the chicken salad**
In a bowl, combine the reserved lemon zest and juice, fennel, green onion, ¾ teaspoon tarragon, mayonnaise, ¾ teaspoon salt, and pepper to taste. Mix until smooth. Chop the chicken finely. Add to the fennel mixture and toss until thoroughly blended. Spoon a generous tablespoon of the salad onto each crostini, garnish with tarragon, and serve.

French or sourdough baguette, 28 slices, each about ½ inch (12 mm) thick

Olive oil, 2 tablespoons

Salt and freshly ground pepper

Lemon, 1

Skinless, boneless chicken breasts, 2, about ¾ lb (375 g) total weight, pounded lightly to an even thickness and patted dry

Canola oil, 1 tablespoon

Fennel bulb, ½, trimmed, quartered lengthwise, and finely chopped

Green (spring) onion, 1, white and pale green parts only, finely chopped

Fresh tarragon, ¾ teaspoon finely chopped, plus more for garnish

Mayonnaise, ⅓ cup (3 fl oz/ 90 ml)

MAKES 28 CROSTINI

75

make more
to store

flatbread with rosemary & olive oil

YEAST DOUGH

Flour, 3½ cups (17½ oz/ 545 g)

Instant yeast, 2¼ teaspoons (1 packet)

Sugar, 1 tablespoon

Salt, 1 tablespoon

Warm water (110°F/43°C), 1¼–1½ cups (10–12 fl oz/ 310–372 ml)

Olive oil, 2 tablespoons

Coarse cornmeal, 1 tablespoon

Olive oil, 2 tablespoons

Fresh rosemary, 2 teaspoons, finely chopped

Coarse sea salt

MAKES 12 PIECES

makes 2 balls dough total

This easy-to-mix yeast dough comes together quickly in the food processor. This recipe makes enough dough for rosemary flatbread, plus the pizza, spinach calzone, and pissaladiére recipes that follow.

1 Make the dough
In a food processor, combine the flour, yeast, sugar, and salt and pulse to blend. Add the water and olive oil and pulse until the dough comes together. Turn the dough out onto a lightly floured surface. Knead the dough for 1–2 minutes to form a smooth ball. Place the dough in an oiled large bowl, turn to coat, and cover with plastic wrap. Let rise in a warm place until doubled in bulk and very spongy, about 1½ hours.

2 Divide the dough
Turn the dough out onto a lightly floured surface, punch down, and knead into a smooth cylinder. Divide into 2 equal pieces and knead again to form 2 smooth balls, dusting with flour if needed. Cover with a kitchen towel and let rest for 10 minutes. Store 1 ball for future use (see Storage Tip, right).

3 Bake the flatbread
Preheat oven to 450°F (230°C). Sprinkle the cornmeal evenly over an 11-by-17-inch (28-by-43-cm) rimmed baking sheet. Place the dough on the prepared pan. Press down on the center, and push and stretch the dough to the edges of the pan evenly. Cover with a damp towel and let rise for 15 minutes. Make several dimples in the dough. Drizzle the dough with the olive oil and sprinkle with the rosemary and sea salt. Bake until golden brown, 15–18 minutes. Cut into pieces and serve.

storage tip

Place each ball separately
in a resealable plastic bag and
refrigerate until ready to use,
up to overnight. Return to room
temperature before proceeding
with the recipe. If freezing, wrap
the dough in plastic wrap before
placing in the bags and freeze
for up to 2 months. To thaw, place
on a plate at room temperature;
until the dough reaches room
temperature and begins to rise
again, about 3 hours.

cook's tip

Vary the pizza topping by using
cured meats such as salami or
pepperoni. Or, substitute other
quick-cooking, freshly cut
vegetables, like bell peppers
(capsicums) or mushrooms.

pesto & cherry tomato pizza

1 **Shape the dough**
Sprinkle the cornmeal evenly over an 11-by-17-inch (28-by-43-cm) rimmed baking sheet. Place the dough on the prepared pan. Very firmly press down on the center, and, working from the center outward, push and stretch the dough to the edges of the pan to achieve an even thickness. (If the dough is difficult to handle, set it aside, covered, for 10 minutes.) Cover with a kitchen towel and let rise for at least 15 minutes.

2 **Assemble and bake the pizza**
Place a rack in the lower third of the oven and preheat to 450°F (230°C). Spread the dough evenly with the pesto, leaving a ¼-inch (6-mm) border uncovered. Arrange the mozzarella and tomatoes evenly over the pesto. Season with salt and pepper. Bake until the edges are golden brown and the cheese is bubbling, 15–18 minutes. Cut into serving pieces and serve warm.

Yeast Dough (page 78),
1 ball, at room temperature

Coarse cornmeal,
1 tablespoon

Pesto, ½ cup (4 fl oz/ 125 ml)

Fresh mozzarella, ½ lb (250 g), sliced

Cherry tomatoes, 1 cup (6 oz/185 g) quartered

Salt and freshly ground pepper

MAKES ABOUT 8 PIECES

pancetta, ricotta & spinach calzone

Yeast Dough (page 78),
1 ball, at room tempertature

Pancetta, ¼ lb (125 g),
coarsely chopped

Whole-milk ricotta cheese,
⅔ cup (5 oz/155 g)

Baby spinach, 1 cup
(2 oz/60 g) finely chopped

**Salt and freshly ground
pepper**

Egg, 1, whisked with
2 teaspoons water

MAKES 12 CALZONE

1 Make the filling
On a lightly floured surface, use your hands to roll the dough into cylinder 12 inches (30 cm) long. Cut into 12 equal pieces, and roll each piece into a smooth ball. Cover with a kitchen towel and let rest at room temperature for 20 minutes. Meanwhile, in a heavy frying pan over medium-low heat, cook the pancetta, stirring occasionally, until crisp, about 4 minutes. Using a slotted spoon, transfer to a paper towel to drain. In a bowl, stir together the pancetta, ricotta, spinach, ½ teaspoon salt, and ¼ teaspoon pepper.

2 Assemble and bake the calzone
Place a rack in the lower third of the oven and preheat to 450°F (230°C). On a lightly floured surface, roll out each dough ball into a round 5–6 inches (13–15 cm) in diameter and ⅛ inch (3 mm) thick. Divide the filling among the center of each round and brush the edges of the dough with water. Lift the edges, stretching and adjusting the dough and compacting the filling, so the edges meet in the center. Firmly crimp the edges and transfer each calzone to a baking sheet lined with parchment (baking) paper, so that the crimped edge and one side is in contact with the pan. Cut a small steam vent in the center of the top. Brush the tops of the calzone with the egg mixture. Bake until golden brown, about 15 minutes. Transfer to a wire rack and let cool for about 5 minutes, then serve.

cook's tip

If desired, serve the calzone
on a platter with a small bowl
of heated marinara sauce in
the center for dipping. Look for
a good-quality, jarred marinara
sauce at an Italian market
or well-stocked supermarket.

cook's tip

You can pit olives quickly using the back of a large chef's knife. Put the olives on a cutting board and lay the widest part of the blade on top, with the sharp edge facing away from you. Carefully roll the olives, pressing down on the blade. The olives should split, allowing you to remove the pits easily.

olive & onion pissaladière

1 Cook the onions

In a large frying pan over medium heat, warm the olive oil. Add the onions and season generously with salt and pepper. Cover and cook gently, stirring every 5 minutes or so, until tender and golden, about 20 minutes.

2 Shape the dough

Meanwhile, sprinkle the cornmeal evenly over an 11-by-17-inch (28-by-43-cm) rimmed baking sheet. Place the dough ball on the prepared pan. Very firmly press down on the center, and, working from the center outward, push and stretch the dough to the edges of the pan to achieve an even thickness. (If the dough is difficult to handle, set it aside, covered, for 10 minutes.) Cover with a kitchen towel and let rise for 15 minutes.

3 Assemble and bake the pissaladière

Place a rack in the lower third of the oven and preheat to 450°F (230°C). Spread the onion mixture over the dough, leaving a ¼-inch (6-mm) border uncovered. Scatter the anchovies and olives over the dough. Bake until the edges are golden brown, 15–18 minutes. Let stand for 3–5 minutes. Cut in half lengthwise and then crosswise into small serving pieces. Serve warm.

Yeast Dough (page 78), 1 ball, at room temperature

Olive oil, ¼ cup (2 fl oz/ 60 ml)

Yellow onions, 1 ½ lb (750 g), halved and sliced thinly

Salt and freshly ground pepper

Coarse cornmeal, 1 tablespoon

Canned anchovy fillets, 8, soaked in warm water for 5 minutes, drained, patted dry, and chopped

Niçoise or other brine-cured black olives, 8, pitted and roughly chopped

MAKES ABOUT
16 PIECES

tomato & fontina tart

SAVORY TART DOUGH

Flour, 3½ cups (17½ oz/ 545 g)

Salt, ½ teaspoon

Unsalted butter, 1 cup (8 oz/250 g), cubed

Eggs, 2, lightly beaten

Lemon juice, 1 tablespoon

Ice water, ¼ cup (2 fl oz/ 60 ml), or more if needed

Shallots, 2, halved lengthwise and thinly sliced

Plum (Roma) tomatoes, 3 large, cut into slices ¼ inch (6 mm) thick

Salt and freshly ground pepper

Fontina cheese, 3 oz (90 g), thinly sliced

Egg yolk, 1, whisked with 1 teaspoon milk

Fresh basil, 2 tablespoons finely chopped (optional)

MAKES ONE 9-INCH (23-CM) TART

makes 2 disks savory tart dough total

This recipe yields enough flaky, buttery, dough to make a delicious and summery tomato tart, the ham and spinach quiches, mascarpone tarts, or rich beef emapananas on the following pages.

1 **Make the dough**
In a food processor, combine the flour, salt, and butter. Pulse until the mixture forms coarse crumbs. In a small bowl, whisk together the eggs, lemon juice, and ¼ cup ice water. With the motor running, quickly add the egg mixture and process just until the dough comes together. Turn out onto a lightly floured surface and form into a smooth cylinder. Cut in half and shape into 2 thick disks. Refrigerate 1 disk and wrap 1 disk for future use (see Storage Tip, right).

2 **Roll out the dough**
Preheat the oven to 375°F (190°C). Roll out the disk of dough into a rough 12 inch (30 cm) round or square. Fold the dough round in half and transfer to a 9-inch (23-cm) round or square tart pan. Unfold the round and ease it into the pan, patting it firmly into the bottom and building up the sides.

3 **Assemble and bake the tart**
Arrange the tomatoes and shallots in the pan. Season with salt and pepper, and top with the cheese. Brush the egg mixture over the crust. Bake until the crust has browned and the cheese has melted, 35–45 minutes. Let cool briefly on a wire rack. Garnish with the basil, if using. Serve warm.

storage tip

If you are planning to use one or both pieces of dough right away, first wrap them securely in plastic wrap and refrigerate for at least 30 minutes. Or, place one or both of the wrapped disks inside a resealable plastic bag and freeze for up to 3 months. To use, the dough must be defrosted at room temperature until workable but still slightly chilled, about 2½ hours.

cook's tip

Stay one step ahead and line
the miniature muffin pans with
dough. Wrap the pans tightly
with plastic wrap, and freeze for
up to 1 month. Let thaw at room
temperature for up to 1 hour
before filling and baking. Bake
the quiches as directed in Step 3.

ham & spinach
quiches

1 Roll out the dough

On a lightly floured surface, roll out the dough disk into a rough round ⅛ inch (3 mm) thick. Using a 2-inch (5-cm) biscuit cutter, cut out as many rounds as possible. Ease the rounds gently into the cups of 1 or 2 miniature muffin pans. The bottoms of the dough should remain rounded, and the edges should be flush with the rim of the pan. Gather the scraps, roll out ⅛ inch thick, and cut out additional rounds. You should have 24 lined cups.

2 Make the filling

Preheat the oven to 400°F (200°C). In a frying pan over low heat, melt the butter. Add the shallots and cook, stirring occasionally, until softened, about 5 minutes. Raise the heat to medium-low, add the spinach, and cook, stirring constantly, until wilted, about 1 minute. In a large measuring cup, whisk together the egg, cream, mustard, ½ teaspoon salt, and a pinch of pepper. Add the spinach mixture, bell pepper, ham, and cheese, and stir to combine. Divide the filling among the lined cups.

3 Bake the quiches

Bake until the quiches are puffy and golden brown, about 20 minutes. Let cool in the pan on a rack for about 10 minutes. Run a knife around the sides of each cup and carefully lift out the quiches. Arrange on a platter and serve.

Savory Tart Dough (page 86), 1 disk

Unsalted butter, 1½ tablespoons

Shallots, 2, finely chopped

Baby spinach, 1 cup (2 oz/60 g) coarsely chopped

Egg, 1

Heavy (double) cream, ⅔ cup (5 fl oz/160 ml)

Dijon mustard, ½ teaspoon

Salt and freshly ground pepper

Red bell pepper (capsicum), 2 tablespoons finely chopped

Ham, 1 oz (30 g), chopped

Gruyère cheese, 2 oz (60 g), finely grated

MAKES 24 SMALL QUICHES

mushroom & mascarpone tartlets

Savory Tart Dough (page 86), 1 disk

Unsalted butter, 1 tablespoon

Olive oil, 2 tablespoons

Leeks, 2 large, including pale green parts, halved, rinsed, and thinly sliced

Cremini, shiitake, or oyster mushrooms, ¾ lb (375 g), trimmed and thinly sliced

Dried porcini mushrooms, ½ oz (15 g), soaked in hot water for 20 minutes, squeezed dry, and finely chopped (optional)

Salt and freshly ground pepper

Mascarpone cheese, ⅔ cup (5 oz/155 g)

MAKES ABOUT
32 SMALL BITES

1 Bake the tart bases
Preheat the oven to 375°F (190°C). Divide the dough disk in half, keeping one half in the refrigerator until needed. On a lightly floured surface, roll out each half into a rough round ⅛ inch (3 mm) thick. Using a 2-inch (5-cm) biscuit cutter, cut out as many rounds as possible. Transfer to 1 or 2 baking sheets. Gather the scraps, roll out ⅛ inch thick, and cut out additional rounds. You should have about 32 rounds. Pierce the rounds in several places with a fork. Bake until the tart bases are slightly golden, about 15 minutes. Transfer to wire racks to cool.

2 Cook the mushrooms
Meanwhile, in a large frying pan over medium heat, melt the butter with the oil. Add the leeks and cook, stirring frequently, until softened, 5–6 minutes. Add the fresh mushrooms and rehydrated porcini (if using), season generously with salt and pepper, and cook, stirring occasionally, until the mushrooms have released their liquid and become dry and softened, about 5 minutes.

3 Assemble the tarts
Spread a generous teaspoon of the mascarpone on each tart base. Mound 2 teaspoons of the mushroom mixture on the cheese. Arrange on a platter and serve at once.

cook's tip

If mascarpone is unavailable, you can approximate its flavor and consistency by whisking ⅓ cup (2½ oz/75 g) softened cream cheese with ⅓ cup sour cream (2½ oz/75 g) until smooth.

cook's tip

The empanada filling can
be made with ground
(minced) turkey, pork, veal
or a combination. This
recipe can easily be doubled
and will keep in an airtight
container for up to 3 days.

beef empanadas

1 Make the filling

In a large, heavy frying pan over medium heat, cook the beef and the pine nuts, stirring to break up the meat, until the beef is no longer pink, about 6 minutes. Using a slotted spoon, transfer to a bowl. Add the onion to the pan over medium heat and cook, stirring occasionally, until softened, about 5 minutes. Add the tomato paste and wine and cook, stirring occasionally, until the mixture is thick and dry, about 3 minutes. Add the currants to the beef mixture along with ¼ teaspoon salt, ¼ teaspoon pepper, the cumin, and oregano. Mix well and adjust the seasoning if necessary.

2 Roll out the dough

Preheat the oven to 375°F (190°C). Line 2 baking sheets with parchment (baking) paper. Divide the dough disk in half, keeping one half in the refrigerator until needed. On a lightly floured surface, roll out each half into a rough round just less than ¼ inch (6 mm) thick. Using a 3-inch (7.5-cm) biscuit cutter, cut out as many rounds as possible. Transfer to the prepared baking sheets. Gather the scraps, roll out, and cut out additional rounds. You should have about 24 rounds. Brush them with the egg mixture.

3 Assemble and bake the empanadas

Place a generous tablespoon of the filling in the center of each dough round. Lift the edges of each round so they meet in the center, compacting the filling. Firmly crimp the edges and transfer the empanadas to a prepared sheet. Press the top edges with a fork. Brush the tops of the empanadas with the egg mixture. Bake until golden brown, about 30 minutes.

Savory Tart Dough (page 86), 1 disk

Lean ground (minced) beef, 6 oz (185 g)

Pine nuts, 3 tablespoons coarsely chopped

Yellow onion, ½, finely chopped

Tomato paste, 1 tablespoon

Red wine, ¼ cup (2 fl oz/ 60 ml)

Currants, 3 tablespoons

Salt and freshly ground pepper

Ground cumin, ½ teaspoon

Dried oregano, ¼ teaspoon

Egg, 1, whisked with 1 tablespoon water

MAKES ABOUT
24 EMPANADAS

the smarter cook

The first step to becoming a smarter cook—one who spends less time in the kitchen but still turns out delicious dishes—is building a collection of inspired small-plate recipes that will jump-start your weekly menu planning. Once you know what you'll be cooking, you can check your pantry and refrigerator, write down your shopping list, and then make just a few strategic trips to the grocery store during the week. These simple efforts will yield satisfying dishes in record time, whether you're feeding your family or entertaining friends.

With a well-stocked pantry and weekly menus, you'll have the foundation for both the meals you plan and the impromptu entertaining you enjoy. In the following pages, you'll find tips on how to make the most of your time and stock your kitchen along with ideas for easy meals and parties.

get started

If you plan your weekly recipes and keep a well-stocked pantry and refrigerator, you'll save time in the kitchen. Use the simple strategies outlined here to put together menus, organize your shopping trips, and get the most out of your hands-on cooking time. Then, even when your days are jam-packed with work and other activities, you'll still find time to entertain your friends and family.

plan ahead

When you take the time to write down your menu ideas before you head to the store, you're able to stock your kitchen with much of what you'll need for the days ahead. That means fewer shopping trips during the busy work and school week. Careful planning also helps you think about how to turn leftovers into tasty second meals.

- **Look at your upcoming get togethers.** Keep your schedule in mind as you plan. If you're hosting a weeknight book club, pick out a few easy recipes that can be assembled quickly or prepped the night before. For fancier affairs—a formal dinner, a holiday cocktail party—consider more elaborate preparations and specialty ingredients. Read through the recipes you've chosen to see if you need to marinate or chill anything ahead of time, or if a dish can be made in advance.

- **Let the seasons be your guide.** Put together party menus that suit the weather: lighter plates with plenty of fresh vegetables in the spring and summer, and heartier, richer fare when the days turn cold.

- **Cook on the weekend.** Take time on the weekend to prepare dishes that will keep for a few days, like dips and sauces. Have your refrigerator stocked with tasty basics that can be easily put together for quick snacks and simple first courses.

- **Plan for leftovers.** Making a batch of white bean dip for a party? Prepare a double batch and use the rest as a sandwich spread. Extra raw vegetables, such as carrot, celery, or jicama sticks; cucumber and bell pepper (capsicum) slices; or trimmed radishes, make great snacks.

THINK SEASONALLY

spring As the days get warmer and fresh herbs and vegetables appear in the market, lighten your fare with radishes, baby carrots, young lettuces, sugar snap peas, and new potatoes. Try using jicama, instead of bread or crackers, as a base for toppings.

summer Make the most of summer's bounty with garden-fresh treats like sun-ripened tomatoes, bunches of leafy basil, fresh figs, sweet stone fruits, and shiny eggplants (aubergines).

autumn Apples, pears, and grapes are at their best in the crisp months of fall. Arrange an assortment of fruits on a cheese platter, or make a fruit compote. Chestnuts, squashes, Brussels sprouts, and hardy greens complement the autumn table.

winter On cold nights, warm up with hearty comfort foods, or enjoy crabs and oysters pulled from chilly waters. Citrus fruits and tropical fruits can add welcome color and tang to the rich foods of winter. Try roasting chestnuts and root vegetables, such as squashes and turnips, and tossing them with a fragrant sage butter.

Prep ahead. A food processor makes speedy work of chopping vegetables and grating cheese. Get in the habit of prepping what you'll need ahead of time. Stored in airtight containers, these ready-to-go ingredients will help cut your work time in half once you start cooking.

Use the right tools. Sharp knives are the key to working quickly and efficiently in the kitchen. A chef's knife and a paring knife are essential. Add a good-quality sauté pan, a grill pan, rimmed baking sheets, and heavy-bottomed saucepans in an assortment of sizes, and you'll be fully equipped to make any of the recipes in this book.

Use the right dishes. Stock up on an assortment of round and square platters and small plates and on such specialty items as a crudité platter and an olive dish. Attractive cocktail napkins, toothpicks, and bamboo skewers are also good to have on hand.

Have your ingredients ready. This step is called *mise en place* (French for "put in place"), and it's the single most important way to save time and reduce stress in the kitchen. Before you begin cooking, measure out all of the ingredients and put them in small bowls, so they're ready to go.

Clean as you go. Before you begin, start out with a clean kitchen—an empty dishwasher, uncluttered countertops, fresh dish towels. Wash pots, pans, and utensils as you cook, to save cleanup time after you eat.

make the most of your time

Once you've laid out your cooking plan, you can start thinking about how to make the most of your time. Getting your shopping and prep work done in advance means you'll spend less hands-on time in the kitchen, leaving you more time for other activities.

- **Stock up.** Avoid last-minute grocery trips by keeping your pantry well stocked. Have a notepad or whiteboard handy in the kitchen, so you can write down any staples that are getting low and replace them promptly. Always keep a good supply of basic nonperishable ingredients on hand. They'll come in handy when you need to improvise simple appetizers, first courses, and snacks.

- **Shop less.** Write down your shopping list as you make out your cooking plan for the week, so that you can pick up all the staples that you'll need in one trip. If you know that you'll be pressed for time on weekdays, stock up on meat and poultry during your big shopping trip, and portion out, wrap, and freeze what you won't be using within a couple days.

- **Do it ahead.** Prep as much as you can when you have extra time. Wash, peel, and chop vegetables, and store them in resealable plastic bags or airtight containers. Skewer meat kebabs, wrap tightly, and refrigerate. Make up marinades or dips and store in the refrigerator. Check your ingredients and tools the night before, so you'll be able to find everything easily when you start to cook.

- **Double up.** Reheated leftovers can be a great help to the busy cook. But don't serve a reheated version of the same dish the next night. Instead of doubling the whole recipe, just cook the foundation, without the accompanying sauce or added flavorings, and finish in a new way.

- **Cook smarter.** Read through the recipe from start to finish before you begin. Visualize the techniques and go through the recipe step by step in your mind. Clear your counters and make sure the kitchen is clean and neat before you start. If you have friends or family around to help, assign them tasks to save time, whether it's peeling carrots, making a salad, or setting the table.

make a meal out of it

Many of these small plates can become the centerpiece of a lunch or dinner menu. Once you have decided which delicious recipe to make for your main dish, you can choose from among a variety of quick and easy side dishes to complete the meal.

- **Salad** To save time, buy packaged, prewashed greens. Choose salad ingredients that complement the dish you are making: a salad with lettuce, cucumbers, and lime-cilantro dressing to accompany quesadillas filled with chorizo (page 37), or an arugula (rocket), tomato, and shaved Parmesan salad dressed with olive oil and lemon juice to serve with calzone (page 83). Make extra dressing and store it in the refrigerator for use on other salads throughout the week.

- **Couscous** Instant couscous, available plain or in a variety of seasoned blends, takes less than 10 minutes to prepare on the stove top. Serve with lamb meatballs (page 55).

- **Potatoes** Buy small potatoes, coat them with olive oil, season with salt, and then roast them as you would other vegetables (see below). Or, boil larger potatoes in salted water for 20–30 minutes, slice, toss with vinaigrette and serve with shrimp skewers (page 52).

- **Tomatoes** Slice ripe tomatoes, arrange the slices on a platter, and season them with olive oil, salt, and freshly ground pepper. If desired, sprinkle with crumbled feta cheese, olives, or chopped fresh herbs.

- **Roasted vegetables** In the time it takes to put together the main ingredients of your meal, you can also roast vegetables. Start with precut fresh produce, such as broccoli and cauliflower florets, butternut squash, or asparagus spears. Toss the vegetables in olive oil and roast on a baking sheet at 400°F (200°C) for 10–30 minutes (depending on the vegetable), stirring occasionally. Season with salt and pepper and serve.

- **Easy desserts** For nights when you want to serve dessert, try these two quick ideas: seasonal fresh fruit drizzled with honey and yogurt, or ice cream topped with caramel sauce and toasted pecans.

SHORTCUT INGREDIENTS

tapenade This pungent spread, made from minced black olives and seasoned with garlic, is delicious lightly spread on toasted baguette slices.

pesto Look for freshly made versions of this vibrant summery sauce at Italian delicatessens, or stock up on flavorful jarred or frozen varieties. Spread on thin toasted baguette slices and top with sliced plum (Roma) tomatoes. Or, toss with freshly cooked spaghetti for an easy weeknight meal.

caponata Available in jars in Italian specialty shops and some supermarkets, this chunky, sweet-and-sour Sicilian mixture of eggplant (aubergine), onion, celery, pine nuts, currants, vinegar, and sugar makes a good summertime dip or bruschetta base. It can also be tossed with hot pasta for an easy sauce.

smoked fish Vacuum-packed smoked salmon and trout can be kept unopened in the refrigerator for several weeks. Serve with a dab of sour cream or crème fraîche on toast points, homemade or packaged blini, or triangles of dense German-style rye or pumpernickel bread.

hummus Look in the refrigerator section of your supermarket for premade hummus. Make a quick sandwich or wrap filling with extra lemon juice, olive oil, salt, minced garlic, and a pinch of cumin. Or, top with a swirl of olive oil and serve with warmed pita triangles, purchased tortilla chips, or crudités such as broccoli florets, carrot sticks, or zucchini spears.

sample dinner menus

Here are some ideas on how to create a satisfying supper by adding one or two side dishes to whatever small-plate recipe you decide to make. When designing your own menus, keep in mind that sauteed vegetables or a salad is usually all you need. You can also double the small-plate recipe or serve two different dishes for the same meal.

IN MINUTES	WEEKEND SUPPERS	FIT FOR COMPANY
Chorizo & Cheese Quesadillas (page 37)	**Beef Empanadas (page 93)**	**Crab Salad with Endive (page 34)**
Pinto beans with oregano	Fried plantains	Chilled cucumber soup
Chips & guacamole	Mixed greens with creamy lime vinaigrette	Cracked pepper crackers
Caprese Skewers (page 26)	**Fritto Misto (page 59)**	**Lamb Meatballs with Cilantro Raita (page 55)**
Rotisserie chicken	Steamed artichokes with melted butter	Spinach salad with feta & almonds
Warm focaccia with fresh thyme & olive oil	Tomato slices with sea salt & olive oil	Toasted whole-wheat pita
Salmon & Herbed Cheese Pinwheels (page 22)	**Grilled Pork with Pineapple Salsa (page 51)**	**Potato Pancakes with Smoked Salmon (page 60)**
Shaved zucchini with Parmesan	Spicy black beans	Butter lettuce with Champagne vinaigrette
Tomato slices with sea salt & olive oil	Steamed rice	Sautéed green beans
Turkey & Manchego Sandwiches (page 30)	**Tamarind-Glazed Chicken Wings (page 64)**	**Tomato & Fontina Tart (page 86)**
Fresh fruit salad	Roasted new potatoes	Arugula & Parmesan salad with citrus vinaigrette
Thai Lettuce Cups (page 29)	Iceburg lettuce wedge with blue cheese dressing	**Shrimp Skewers with Basil Oil (page 52)**
Cucumber & red onion salad	**Pesto & Cherry Tomato Pizza (page 81)**	Orzo pasta with lemon
Rice noodles with cilantro & rice wine vinagrette	Radicchio salad with pancetta & Parmesan	Grilled asparagus

easy appetizers

Speed and ease characterize all of these small plates, any one of which would be perfect when you are short on time and guests are coming.

- **Precut vegetables & fruit** If you're pressed for time, supermarkets now stock a wide variety of prewashed, precut fruits and vegetables, which can come in handy for putting together last-minute crudité or dessert platters.

- **Cheese puffs** For hot, elegant bites, wrap small squares or triangles of store-bought puff pastry around a piece of cheese and a pinch of fresh herbs, such as thyme, and bake in a 375°F (190°C) oven until golden, about 20 minutes. For cheese straws, roll out a sheet of puff pastry, brush with egg white, sprinkle with Parmesan, and fold in half into a rectangle. Cut crosswise into strips 1 inch (2.5 cm) wide, turn the ends to twist the strips, and place on a baking sheet. Bake in a 375°F (190°C) oven until puffed and golden, about 20 minutes.

- **Snack mixes** Look in the Asian food section of your supermarket for Japanese snack mixes—shiny mixtures of tiny, crunchy, puffed rice crackers (some wrapped with a strip of nori—the same seaweed used in sushi rolls) and crunchy dried peas dipped in fiery wasabi.

- **Cheese platter** Put together a platter of your favorite cheeses such as young *crottin* (goat cheese), Reblochon (semisoft cow's milk cheese), and Roquefort (blue sheep's milk cheese). Scatter with Marcona almonds—smooth, buttery Spanish almonds that are a welcome change from the usual mixed nuts—then add slices of ripe pears, red grapes, and a block of quince paste (*membrillo*). Serve with toasted baguette slices and crackers.

- **Charcuterie** Arrange cured meats, such as salami, prosciutto, and hot coppa, and thick slices of country-style pâté on a decorative cutting board or platter. Garnish the board with radishes and cornichons, and place a ramekin of grainy mustard for spreading alongside. Serve with toasted baguette slices (page 70).

PARTY TIPS

make batches Make a double batch of your favorite recipes or dishes that you think will be popular with guests. Have the extras arranged on plates in the refrigerator, so you can easily replenish your platters.

keep it fresh Replenish smaller plates frequently. They look tidier and more appealing that a single large platter.

circulate new dishes Time new dishes one or two at a time throughout the party. It will boost interest and keep items from wilting or drying out before they are eaten.

leave space Make sure there's enough room on the platter for guests to easily remove what they want.

keep it natural Lemon, chard leaves and kale, cucumber slices, and fresh flat-leaf parsley and dill sprigs all make appealing garnishes or food-friendly beds for appetizer platters. Look for particularly pretty herbs, such as blossoming chives or purple basil.

be creative Think of new ways to serve your appetizers. Present creamy single bites such as lemon chicken salad in attractive oversized silver spoons. Serve chilled soups in slim cordial or shot glasses, and hot soups in demitasse or espresso cups.

set out extras Put out small bowls of nuts, such as cashews, almonds, and pistachios; candied walnuts; dried fruits, such as apricots; and crackers or chips for easy bites.

sample party menus

Use these menus to help you plan parties for the special occasions in your life. Never try to make more recipes than you can easily cook or serve, and always include dishes that you can prepare partly or fully in advance. And don't forget that high-quality purchased items are a good way to cut down on kitchen time.

ASIAN-THEMED PARTY	HOLIDAY OPEN HOUSE	ALFRESCO IN TUSCANY
Thai Lettuce Cups (page 29)	**Spiced Roasted Nuts** (page 25)	**Ricotta, Fig & Prosciutto Bruschetta** (page 18)
Spring Rolls with Lime-Cilantro Sauce (page 48)	**Crostini with Steak & Horseradish Cream** (page 44)	**Polenta with Eggplant Pesto** (page 71)
Prepared sushi rolls	**Roasted Dates with Parmesan & Bacon** (page 63)	**Peaches with Prosciutto & Mint** (page 41)
Asian snack mix	Chocolate truffles	**Antipasto platter with salumi, Italian cheeses, and *grissini***
Saketinis, lychee martinis, Asian beer	*Champagne, hot mulled cider, microbrewed holiday ales*	Mixed olives
		Prosecco, Pinot Grigio

LATIN FIESTA	BOOK CLUB NIGHT	TAILGATE PARTY
Grilled Pork with Pineapple Salsa (page 51)	**Pear Compote with Cheeses** (page 14)	**Turkey & Manchego Sandwiches** (page 30)
Guacamole & Sweet Potato Chips (page 47)	**White Bean Dip with Pita** (page 17)	**Tamarind-Glazed Chicken Wings** (page 64)
Beef Empanadas (page 93)	**Lemon Chicken Salad on Crostini** (page 75)	**Pesto & Cherry Tomato Pizza** (page 81)
Mexican beer, margaritas, Caipirinhas	Assorted crackers	*Hot mulled cider, beer*
	Sauvignon Blanc, beer	

the well-stocked kitchen

Successful entertaining is all about being prepared. If your pantry, refrigerator, and freezer are well stocked and organized, you'll save time in the kitchen when you are ready to cook. If you always know what you have on hand and what you need to buy, you'll make fewer trips to the grocery store, and shop more efficiently while you're there. On the following pages, you'll find easy-to-use lists of the ingredients you'll need to make the recipes in this book.

You'll also discover dozens of tips on how to keep foods fresh and store them properly. Use this information to check on what you already have and what you need to buy when you go shopping. The time you spend organizing your kitchen will pay off whenever unexpected guests arrive or you need to turn a small plate into a satisfying family supper.

the pantry

The pantry is one or more cupboards or a closet in which you keep dried herbs and spices, pastas and grains, beans, nuts, oils and vinegars, and fresh foods that don't need refrigeration, such as onions, potatoes, and garlic. It must be cool and dry and should be dark when not in use. Heat and light are enemies of freshness, drying out herbs and spices and hastening rancidity in grains, nuts, and oils.

stock your pantry

- Take inventory of what is in your pantry using the Pantry Staples list.

- Remove everything from the pantry; clean the shelves and reline with paper, if needed; and then resort items by type.

- Discard items that have passed their expiration date or have a stale or otherwise questionable appearance.

- Make a list of items you need to replace or stock.

- Shop for items on your list.

- Restock the pantry, organizing items by type so they are easy to find.

- Write the purchase date on perishable items and label bulk items.

- Keep staples you use often toward the front of the pantry.

- Keep dried herbs and spices in separate containers and preferably in separate spice or herb organizer, shelf, or drawer.

keep it organized

- Look over the recipes in your weekly plan, and check your pantry to make sure you have all the ingredients you'll need.

- Rotate items as you use them, moving the oldest ones to the front of the pantry so they will be used first.

- Keep a list of the items you use up so that you can replace them.

WINES & SPIRITS

Always keep a supply of good-quality wines, spirits, and mixers on hand, so you don't have to run to the store when friends arrive unexpectedly. For serving, arrange the wines and spirits on a flat surface alongside a few traditional mixers, a selection of glasses, some ice cubes, and a stack of coasters. If serving white wine, keep it cool in an ice bucket.

WINES
- Sparkling wine or champagne
- Sauvignon Blanc
- Rosé
- Pinot Noir
- Zinfandel

SPIRITS
- Vodka
- Gin
- Tequila
- Dark rum

MIXERS
- Soda water
- Tonic water
- Cranberry juice
- Cola

PANTRY STORAGE

Keep pantry items in small quantities so you restock regularly, ensuring freshness.

dried herbs & spices Always store herbs and spices in a cool place away from direct heat, such as a stove top. Heat will cause them to dry out, losing their volatile oils that provide flavor. Even many properly dried seasonings lose potency after 6 months. Shop for herbs and spices in ethnic markets and natural-foods stores, where they are often sold in bulk and are usually cheaper and of higher quality.

oils Store unopened bottles of oil on a cool, dark shelf for up to 1 year. Once opened, store at room temperature for 3 months or in the refrigerator for as long as 6 months. Smell oil before using to make sure it has not developed any off odors, which can be a sign of rancidity.

grains & pastas Store grains and pastas in airtight containers. Grains will keep for up to 3 months; unopened pastas will keep for up to 1 year. Once opened, use pasta within 6 months.

fresh foods Store in a cool, dark place and check occasionally for sprouting or spoilage. Keep potatoes in a loosely closed paper bag to shield them from direct light, which can cause their skins to turn green.

canned foods Discard canned foods if the can shows any signs of buckling or expansion. Once you have opened a can, transfer unused contents to an airtight container and store in the refrigerator or freezer.

PANTRY STAPLES

GRAINS & PASTAS

cornmeal

flour

instant or pre-cooked polenta

rice vermicelli

DRIED HERBS & SPICES

black peppercorns

cayenne pepper

cinnamon, ground

cinnamon sticks

cumin, ground

curry powder

fennel seeds

oregano

paprika

red pepper flakes

sage

sesame seeds

star anise

white pepper, ground

NUTS

almonds

walnuts

FRESH FOODS

avocados

garlic

onions (red, sweet, yellow)

potatoes

shallots

sweet potatoes

tomatoes

OILS

Asian sesame oil

canola oil

corn oil

olive oil, pure and extra-virgin

VINEGARS

balsamic vinegar

red wine vinegar

rice vinegar

CONDIMENTS

Asian fish sauce

Dijon mustard

hoisin sauce

horseradish, prepared

mayonnaise

soy sauce

whole-grain mustard

Worcestershire sauce

CANNED & JARRED FOODS

anchovy fillets

cannellini beans

capers

chickpeas (garbanzo beans)

fig jam

green & black olives

honey

oil-packed sun-dried tomatoes

pesto

tamarind paste or concentrate

tapenade

tomato paste

the refrigerator & freezer

Once you have stocked and organized your pantry, you can apply the same time-saving principles to your refrigerator and freezer. Used for short-term cold storage, the refrigerator is ideal for keeping meats, poultry, dairy, vegetables, and leftovers fresh. Proper freezing will preserve most of the flavor in meat, poultry, and many prepared dishes for a few months.

general tips

- Foods lose flavor under refrigeration, so proper storage and an even temperature of below 40°F (5°C) is important.

- Freeze foods at 0°F (-18°C) to retain color, texture, and flavor.

- Don't crowd foods in the refrigerator or freezer. Air should circulate freely to keep foods evenly cooled.

- To prevent freezer burn, use only moistureproof wrappings, such as aluminum foil, airtight plastic containers, or resealable plastic bags.

leftover storage

- For safety, discard any prepared foods that have been at room temperature for 3 hours or longer. Also, discard dips, spreads, and other foods that were shared by guests.

- To store extra food that was never served, wrap it tightly in plastic wrap or put it into an airtight container or resealable plastic bag and refrigerate for up to 4 days.

- Check the contents of the refrigerator at least once a week and promptly discard old or spoiled food.

- Let food cool to room temperature before storing it in the refrigerator or freezer. Transfer the cooled food to an airtight plastic or glass container, leaving room for expansion if freezing. Or, put the cooled food into a resealable plastic freezer bag, expelling as much air as possible before sealing, and then refrigerate or freeze.

KEEP IT ORGANIZED

Once you have stocked and organized your pantry, you should apply the same basic rules to both your refrigerator and your freezer.

clean first Remove items a few at a time and place them on the counter or in the sink. Using a sponge, wash the refrigerator thoroughly with warm, soapy water, then rinse well with clear water. Wash and rinse your freezer at the same time. Replace the contents when you have finished, discarding any items that have been frozen too long.

rotate items Check the expiration dates on refrigerated items and discard any that have exceeded their time. Also, toss out any items that have off odors or look questionable.

stock up Use the Refrigerator Staples list on the opposite page as a starting point to decide what items you need to buy or replace.

shop Shop for the items on your list.

date of purchase Label items that you plan to keep for more than a few weeks, writing the date directly on the package or on a piece of masking tape.

DAIRY

assorted cheeses

eggs

heavy (double) cream

milk

plain yogurt

ricotta cheese

sour cream

unsalted butter

FRUITS & VEGETABLES

arugula (rocket)

Belgian endive (chicory/witloof)

bell peppers (capsicums)

celery

cucumbers

fennel bulbs

green (spring) onions

jalapeño chiles

lemons

limes

mushrooms

peaches

pears

radishes

FRESH HERBS

basil

chives

cilantro (fresh coriander)

flat-leaf (Italian) parsley

mint

oregano

fresh herb & vegetable storage

- Trim the stem ends of a bunch of parsley, stand the bunch in a glass of water, drape a plastic bag loosely over the leaves, and refrigerate. Wrap other fresh herbs in a damp paper towel, slip into a plastic bag, and store in the crisper. Rinse and stem all herbs just before using.

- Store tomatoes and eggplants (aubergines) at room temperature.

- Cut about ½ inch (12 mm) off the end of each asparagus spear; stand the spears, tips up, in a glass of cold water; and refrigerate, changing the water daily. The asparagus will keep for up to 1 week.

- Rinse leafy greens, such as arugula, spin dry in a salad spinner, wrap in damp paper towels, and store in a resealable plastic bag in the crisper for up to a week. In general, store other vegetables in plastic bags in the crisper and rinse before using. Sturdy vegetables will keep for up to a week; more delicate ones will keep for only a few days.

cheese storage

- Wrap all cheeses well to prevent them from drying out. Hard cheeses, such as Parmesan, have a low moisture content, so they keep longer than fresh cheeses, such as feta or *queso fresco*. Use fresh cheeses within a couple days. Store soft and semisoft cheeses for up to 2 weeks and hard cheeses for up to 1 month.

meat & poultry storage

- Use fresh meat and poultry within 2 days of purchase. If using packaged meat, check the expiration date on the package and use before that date.

- To prevent cross-contamination with other foods, always place packaged meats on a plate in the coldest part of the refrigerator (toward the back of the bottom shelf or in a meat drawer). Once you have opened the package, discard the original wrappings and rewrap any unused portions in fresh wrapping.

index

A

Aioli, Lemon, 56
Appetizers
    easy, 100
    sample menus of, 101
Artichokes with Lemon Aioli, 56
Arugula
    storing, 107
Asparagus, 107
Avocados
    Ceviche with Mango and Avocado, 68
    Guacamole a d Sweet Potato Chips, 47

B

Bacon. *See also* Pancetta
    Roasted Dates with Parmesan
        and Bacon, 63
Basil
    Basil Oil, 52
    Caprese Skewers, 26
    Eggplant Pesto, 71
Beans
    Fried Garbanzos, 33
    White Bean Dip with Pita, 17
Beef
    Beef Empanadas, 93
    Crostini with Steak and Horseradish
        Cream, 44
    storing, 107
Belgian endive
    Crab Salad with Endive, 34
    Lemon Chicken Salad on Crostini, 74
Bell peppers
    Grilled Pork with Pineapple Salsa, 51
    Thai Lettuce Cups, 29
    Tomatillo Gazpacho, 72

Bread. *See also* Sandwiches; Tortillas
    Crostini with Eggplant Pesto, 70
    Crostini with Steak and Horseradish
        Cream, 44
    Flatbread with Rosemary and Olive
        Oil, 78
    Lemon Chicken Salad on Crostini, 75
    Pear Compote with Cheeses, 14
    Ricotta, Fig and Prosciutto
        Bruschetta, 18
    Walnut Crostini with Gorgonzola
        and Pear, 10
    White Bean Dip with Pita, 17
Bruschetta, Ricotta, Fig, and Prosciutto, 18

C

Calzone, Pancetta, Ricotta, and
    Spinach, 82
Canned foods
    as pantry staples, 105
    storing, 105
Caponata, 98
Caprese Skewers, 26
Ceviche with Mango and Avocado, 68
Charcuterie, 100
Cheese
    Caprese Skewers, 26
    Cheese Puffs, 100
    Cheese Straws, 100
    Chorizo and Cheese Quesadillas, 37
    Eggplant Pesto, 71
    Goat Cheese Stuffed Tomatoes, 38
    Gruyère-Chive Popovers, 67
    Ham and Spinach Quiches, 89
    Mushroom and Mascarpone
        Tartlets, 90

    Pancetta, Ricotta, and Spinach
        Calzone, 82
    Pear Compote with Cheeses, 14
    platter, 100
    Pesto and Cherry Tomato Pizza, 81
    Ricotta, Fig, and Prosciutto
        Bruschetta, 18
    Roasted Dates with Parmesan
        and Bacon, 63
    Salmon and Herbed Cheese
        Pinwheels, 22
    Smoked Salmon and Cream Cheese
        Sandwich, 31
    storing, 107
    Tomato and Fontina Tart, 86
    Turkey and Manchego Sandwiches, 30
    Walnut Crostini with Gorgonzola
        and Pear, 10
Chicken
    Lemon Chicken Salad on Crostini, 75
    storing, 107
    Tamarind-Glazed Chicken Wings, 64
Chips
    Sweet Potato Chips, 47
    Tortilla Chips, 46
Chorizo and Cheese Quesadillas, 37
Cilantro Raita, 55
Citrus-Marinated Olives, 13
Compote, Pear, with Cheeses, 14
Condiments, 105
Couscous, 98
Crab Salad with Endive, 34
Cream cheese
    Goat Cheese Stuffed Tomatoes, 38
    Salmon and Herbed Cheese
        Pinwheels, 22

Smoked Salmon and Cream Cheese
Sandwich, 31
Crostini
Crostini with Eggplant Pesto, 70
Crostini with Steak and Horseradish
Cream, 44
Lemon Chicken Salad on Crostini, 75
Making, 70
Walnut Crostini with Gorgonzola
and Pear, 10

D
Dairy products, 107
Dates
pitting, 62
Roasted Dates with Parmesan
and Bacon, 63
Desserts, easy, 98
Dips
Guacamole, 47
vegetables with, 16
White Bean Dip with Pita, 17
Dishes, 97

E
Eggplant
caponata, 98
Crostini with Eggplant Pesto, 70
Polenta with Eggplant Pesto, 71
storing, 107
Empanadas
Beef Empanadas, 93
Pork Empanadas, 92
Turkey Empanadas, 92
Veal Empanadas, 92
Equipment, 97

F
Fennel
Crab Salad with Endive, 34
Lemon Chicken Salad on Crostini, 75
Fig, Ricotta, and Prosciutto Bruschetta, 18
Fish
Ceviche with Mango and Avocado, 68
Potato Pancakes with Smoked
Salmon, 60
Salmon and Herbed Cheese
Pinwheels, 22
smoked, 98
Smoked Salmon and Cream
Cheese Sandwich, 31
Flatbread with Rosemary and Olive Oil, 78
Fontina and Tomato Tart, 86
Freezing tips, 106
Fried Garbanzos, 33
Fritto Misto, 59
Fruits. See also individual fruit
precut, 100
storing, 107

G
Garbanzos, Fried, 33
Gazpacho, Tomatillo, 72
Goat Cheese Stuffed Tomatoes, 38
Gorgonzola, Walnut Crostini with Pear
and, 10
Grains
as pantry staples, 105
storing, 105
Greens. See also individual greens
prewashed, packaged, 98
storing, 107
Grilled Pork with Pineapple Salsa, 51

Gruyère-Chive Popovers, 67
Guacamole and Sweet Potato Chips, 47

H
Ham. See also Prosciutto
Ham and Spinach Quiches, 89
Herbs
dried, 105
fresh, 107
as pantry staples, 105
storing, 105, 107
Hummus, 98

K
Knives, 97

L
Lamb
Lamb Meatballs with Cilantro Raita, 55
Leek, Mushroom, and Mascarpone
Tarts, 90
Leftovers
planning for, 96, 97
storing, 106
Lemons
Lemon Aioli, 56
Lemon Chicken Salad on Crostini, 75
as refrigerator staple, 107
Spicy Lemon Dipping Sauce, 58
Lettuce
Smoked Salmon and Cream
Cheese Sandwich, 31
Thai Lettuce Cups, 29
Limes
Ceviche with Mango and Avocado, 68
Lime-Cilantro Sauce, 48

M

Manchego and Turkey Sandwiches, 30

Mango, Ceviche with Avocado and, 68

Mascarpone and Leek Tartlets, 90

Meatballs, Lamb, with Cilantro
   Raita, 55

Menu planning, 96–101

Mise en place, 97

Mozzarella cheese
   Caprese Skewers, 26
   Pesto and Cherry Tomato Pizza, 81

Mushroom and Mascarpone
   Tartlets, 90

N

Noodles. *See* Pasta and noodles

Nuts
   as pantry staples, 105
   Spiced Roasted Nuts, 25

O

Oils
   Basil Oil, 52
   as pantry staples, 105
   Rosemary Oil, 53
   storing, 105

Olives
   Citrus-Marinated Olives, 13

Olive and Onion Pissaladière, 85
   pitting, 84

Oranges
   Citrus-Marinated Olives, 13

P

Pancakes, Potato, with Smoked
   Salmon, 60

Pancetta, Ricotta, and Spinach
   Calzone, 82

Pans, 97

Pantry
   organizing, 104

stocking, 97, 104, 105
   storage tips for, 105

Paprika, 32

Parmesan cheese
   Cheese Straws, 100
   Eggplant Pesto, 71
   Roasted Dates with Parmesan
      and Bacon, 63

Parsley, 107

Parties
   menus for, 101
   tips for, 100

Pasta and noodles
   as pantry staples, 105
   Spring Rolls with Lime-Cilantro
      Sauce, 48
   storing, 105

Peaches
   Peaches with Prosciutto and Mint, 41
   peeling, 40

Pears
   Pear Compote with Cheeses, 14
   Walnut Crostini with Gorgonzola
      and Pear, 10

Pecans
   Spiced Roasted Nuts, 25

Pesto
   Eggplant Pesto, 71
   store-bought, 98

Pineapple Salsa, Grilled Pork with, 51

Pinwheels, Salmon and Herbed
   Cheese, 22

Pissaladière, Olive and Onion, 85

Pita, White Bean Dip with, 17

Pizza, Pesto and Cherry Tomato, 81

Planning, 96–101

Polenta with Eggplant Pesto, 71

Popovers, Gruyère-Chive, 67

Pork. *See also* Bacon; Ham; Pancetta;
   Prosciutto; Sausage
   Grilled Pork with Pineapple Salsa, 51

Pork Empanadas, 92
   storing, 107
   Thai Lettuce Cups, 29

Potatoes
   Potato Pancakes with Smoked
      Salmon, 60
   as pantry staple, 105
   rounding out meal with, 98
   storing, 105

Prep work, 97

Prosciutto
   Peaches with Prosciutto and Mint, 41
   Ricotta, Fig and Prosciutto
      Bruschetta, 18

Puff pastry
   Cheese Puffs, 100
   Cheese Straws, 100

Q

Quesadillas, Chorizo and Cheese, 37

Quiches, Ham and Spinach, 89

R

Radishes with Butter and Sea Salt, 21

Raita, Cilantro, 55

Refrigerating tips, 106–7

Ricotta cheese
   Pancetta, Ricotta, and Spinach
      Calzone, 82
   Ricotta, Fig and Prosciutto
      Bruschetta, 18
   storing, 107

Roasted Dates with Parmesan and
   Bacon, 63

Rosemary Oil, 53

S

Salads
   Crab Salad with Endive, 34
   Lemon Chicken Salad on Crostini, 75
   rounding out meal with, 98

Salmon
    Potato Pancakes with Smoked
      Salmon, 60
    Salmon and Herbed Cheese
      Pinwheels, 22
    Smoked Salmon and Cream
      Cheese Sandwich, 31
Salsa, Pineapple, 51
Salt, sea, 20
Sandwiches
    Smoked Salmon and Cream Cheese
      Sandwich, 31
    Turkey and Manchego Sandwiches, 30
Sauces
    Eggplant Pesto, 71
    Lemon Aioli, 56
    Lime-Cilantro Sauce, 48
    Pineapple Salsa, 51
    Spicy Lemon Dipping Sauce, 58
Sausage
    Chorizo and Cheese Quesadillas, 37
    Thai Lettuce Cups, 29
Savory Tart Dough, 86
    Beef Empanadas, 93
    Ham and Spinach Quiches, 89
    Mushroom and Mascarpone
      Tartlets, 90
    storing, 87
    Tomato and Fontina Tart, 86
Scallops
    Ceviche with Mango and Avocado, 68
Seasons, cooking with, 96
Shopping, 97
Shortcuts, 98
Shrimp
    Fritto Misto, 59
    Shrimp Skewers with Basil Oil, 52
    Spring Rolls with Lime-Cilantro
      Sauce, 48
Skewers
    Caprese Skewers, 26

Grilled Pork with Pineapple Salsa, 51
    Shrimp Skewers with Basil Oil, 52
Smoked Salmon and Cream Cheese
    Sandwich, 31
Snack mixes, 100
Soups. See Gazpacho
Spiced Roasted Nuts, 25
Spices
    as pantry staples, 105
    storing, 105
Spicy Lemon Dipping Sauce, 58
Spinach
    Ham and Spinach Quiches, 89
    Pancetta, Ricotta, and Spinach
      Calzone, 82
Spirits, 104
Spring Rolls with Lime-Cilantro Sauce, 48
Squid
    Fritto Misto, 59
Storage tips, 105
Sweet Potato Chips, Guacamole and, 47

T

Tamarind-Glazed Chicken Wings, 64
Tapenade, 98
Tarts
    Mushroom, Leek, and Mascarpone
      Tarts, 90
    Savory Tart Dough, 86
    Tomato and Fontina Tart, 86
Thai Lettuce Cups, 29
Tomatillo Gazpacho, 72
Tomatoes
    Caprese Skewers, 26
    Goat Cheese Stuffed Tomatoes, 38
    Pesto, and Cherry Tomato Pizza, 81
    rounding out meal with, 98
    storing, 107
    Tomato and Fontina Tart, 86
Tortillas
    Chorizo and Cheese Quesadillas, 37

Salmon and Herbed Cheese
    Pinwheels, 22
Tortilla Chips, 46
Turkey
    storing, 107
    Turkey Empanadas, 92
    Turkey and Manchego Sandwiches, 30

V

Veal
    storing, 107
    Veal Empanadas, 92
Vegetables. See also individual
    vegetables
    with dips, 16
    as pantry staples, 105
    precut, 100
    prepping, 97
    roasted, 98
    rounding out meal with, 98
    storing, 105, 107
Vinegars, 105

W

Walnut Crostini with Gorgonzola and
    Pear, 10
White Bean Dip with Pita, 17
Wines, 104

Y

Yeast Dough, 78
    Flatbread with Rosemary and
      Olive Oil, 78
    Olive and Onion Pissaladière, 85
    Pesto and Cherry Tomato Pizza, 81
    Pancetta, Ricotta, and Spinach
      Calzone, 82
    storing, 79
Yogurt
    Cilantro Raita, 55

Oxmoor
House.

OXMOOR HOUSE

Oxmoor House books are distributed by Sunset Books
80 Willow Road, Menlo Park, CA 94025
Telephone: 650 321 3600 Fax: 650 324 1532

Vice President/General Manager Rich Smeby
National Accounts Manager/Special Sales Brad Moses
Oxmoor House and Sunset Books are divisions of
Southern Progress Corporation

WILLIAMS-SONOMA
Founder & Vice-Chairman Chuck Williams

THE WILLIAMS-SONOMA FOOD MADE FAST SERIES
Conceived and produced by Weldon Owen Inc.
814 Montgomery Street, San Francisco, CA 94133
Telephone: 415 291 0100 Fax: 415 291 8841

In collaboration with Williams-Sonoma, Inc.
3250 Van Ness Avenue, San Francisco, CA 94109

Photographers Tucker & Hossler
Food Stylist Kevin Crafts
Food Stylist's Assistant Alexa Hyman
Text Writer Stephanie Rosenbaum

Library of Congress Cataloging-in-Publication data is available.
ISBN 13: 978-0-8487-3185-4
ISBN 10: 0-8487-3185-9

WELDON OWEN INC.

Chief Executive Officer John Owen
President and Chief Operating Officer Terry Newell
Vice President Sales and New Business Development Amy Kaneko
Vice President and Creative Director Gaye Allen
Vice President and Publisher Hannah Rahill
Senior Art Director Kyrie Forbes Panton
Senior Editor Kim Goodfriend
Associate Editor Lauren Hancock
Senior Designer and Photo Director Andrea Stephany
Designer Britt Staebler
Production Director Chris Hemesath
Color Manager Teri Bell
Production Manager Todd Rechner

A WELDON OWEN PRODUCTION

Copyright © 2007 by Weldon Owen Inc. and Williams-Sonoma, Inc.
All rights reserved, including the right of reproduction in
whole or in part in any form.

Set in Formata
First printed in 2007
10 9 8 7 6 5 4 3 2 1
Color separations by Bright Arts Singapore
Printed by Tien Wah Press

Printed in Singapore

ACKNOWLEDGMENTS
Weldon Owen wishes to thank the following people for their generous support in producing this book:
Heather Belt, Ken DellaPenta, Judith Dunham, Peggy Fallon, Denise Lincoln, and Sharon Silva

Photograph by Bill Bettencourt: page 45 (upper right)

A NOTE ON WEIGHTS AND MEASURES
All recipes include customary U.S. and metric measurements. Metric conversions are based on
a standard developed for these books and have been rounded off. Actual weights may vary.